10. WHISKING BOWL
11. STRAINER
12. PASTRY BRUSH
13. MEASURING JAR

GW00374728

FRESH FRUIT GATEAU

PHOTOGRAPH BY JIGNESH JHAVERI

BAKED DISHES

TARLA DALAL

India's # 1 Cookery Author

S&C

SANJAY & CO.

MUMBAI

Second Printing : 2008

Copyright © Sanjay & Co.

"Tarla Dalal" is also a registered trademark owned by Sanjay & Co.

ISBN 10: 81-89491-39-3

ISBN 13: 978-8-189491-39-0

Price: Rs. 89/-

Published & Distributed by : **Sanjay & Company**

353/A-1, Shah & Nahar Industrial Estate, Dhanraj Mill Compound, Lower Parel (W), Mumbai - 400 013. INDIA.
Tel. : (91-22) 2496 8068 ● Fax : (91-22) 2496 5876 ● E-mail : sanjay@tarladalal.com

---

UK and USA customers can call us on :

UK : 02080029533 ● USA : 213-634-1406

For books, Membership on **tarladalal.com**, Subscription for **Cooking & More** and Recipe queries

Timing : 9.30 a.m. to 7.00 p.m. (IST), from Monday to Saturday

Local call charges applicable

Recipe Research & Production Design	**Nutritionists**	**Photography**	**Designed by**	**Copy Editing**
Arati Fedane	Nisha Katira	Jignesh Jhaveri	Satyamangal Rege	Janani Gopalakrishnan
Umaima Abdulally	Sapna Kamdar			
Vibhuti Punjabi	**Food Styling**	**Typesetting**	**Printed by :**	
Ritika Rajpal	Shubhangi Dhaimade	Adityas Enterprises	Minal Sales Agencies, Mumbai	

BULK PURCHASES : Tarla Dalal Cookbooks are ideal gifts. If you are interested in buying more than 500 assorted copies of Tarla Dalal Cookbooks at special prices, please contact us at 91-22-2496 8068 or email : sanjay@tarladalal.com

INTRODUCTION

'Baked Dish' – This very term reminds us of continental cuisine. There is no denying that it is a very "Western" concept, but it has started making headway into Indian homes and that too at breakneck speed. The reason for the growing popularity of baked dishes could be attributed among other things to the excitement-seeking palates of today's youngsters, or to their desire to cook exotic dishes quickly and easily!

I am sure you would have encountered common baked dishes such as Vegetable Au Gratin and Baked Macaroni sometime in your life. Exciting though they are, the repertoire of baked dishes is in no way limited to these. Different cuisines have their own versions of bakes dishes. For example, the Mexicans have Enchiladas, Italians have Lasagne, and the French have the famous Au Gratin!

Here, I have recorded a lot of traditional all-time favourite recipes from various cultures, including Mexican, Italian and French, as well as innovated and presented various new recipes.

I know that the word 'bake' would immediately have conjured up the image of aromatic cakes, cookies, breads and pies, which delight the sweet tooth, but in this book I have broken away from the stereotype and focused on savoury meal-time baked dishes, which involve Everyday Bakes, Quick Bakes, Party Bakes and Quiches & Pies.

I am sure you are going to enjoy making these dishes, whether it is simple ones like **Minty Baked Potatoes,** page 27 and **Asparagus and Corn Augratin,** page 31 or the more exotic ones like **Fettuccine Spinach Bake,** page 41, **Spicy Mexican Pasta Bake,** page 59, **Baked Cannelloni with Pomodoro Sauce,** page 70 and **Spinach and Corn Quiche,** page 80.

As you browse through the book, you are sure to notice that most of the ingredients are the same for almost all the recipes, but trust me the end-result of each recipe is distinctly different. Just like for cooking *parathas* you have flour, ghee and oil as the basic ingredients, so also with baked dishes you have cheese, cream, white sauce, tomato sauce, and so on. And the quality of these basic ingredients contributes significantly to the success of each dish. Therefore, I have listed ten basic recipes towards the end of the book. It is these that are mixed and matched in various innovative combinations with additional ingredients to give you exciting new flavours.

The diet-conscious among my readers will also be happy to note that I have not forgotten them! Many of the recipes also suggest more healthy alternatives to fat-laden ingredients, to help cut down on the recipes' calorie count.

Hope you enjoy this novel offering of mine and may you bake your way to everybody's heart, through their stomach!

◌ **CONTENTS** ◌

QUICHES & PIES

BASIC RECIPES

A FEW TIPS ON BAKING

1. The baking dish used for baked dishes should be made of an ovenproof material, such as glass or ceramic. The dish should be fairly deep to prevent the bubbling sauce and melting cheese from spilling over into the oven as the dish bakes.

2. Buttering the bottom and sides of the dish helps prevent the ingredients from sticking to the dish when it is baked.

3. A baked dish tastes flat if it is not seasoned properly. Once the dish is assembled, it is tough to alter the seasoning because you can add stuff only on the top and it won't blend with the rest of the dish. So, you need to pay attention to adding salt and pepper as you go along, seasoning the vegetables you're sautéing as well as the white sauce while you're stirring it. Remember to add lots of salt to the water in which you cook the pasta, and a pinch of salt and pepper to the bread crumb topping as well. Each component of your baked pasta should taste wonderful on its own. If it does, you will definitely not wind up with a flat-tasting finished dish.

4. Always remember not to overcook or even completely cook till perfection any of the vegetables since they will be exposed to some heat while baking and will get cooked further. So, always make sure they are precooked only to a level slightly less than perfection.

5. When pre-cooking the pasta for a baked dish, it is important that it is removed from the heat while it is still a little undercooked, otherwise, the additional cooking and liquid absorption during the baking process will cause the pasta to become overdone and mushy. The water should also be completely drained after cooking the pasta, so that the excess moisture is not added to the rest of the dish, causing it to become too watery.

6. There are various varieties of cheese available in the market. I have limited the usage in this book to only the processed/cooking cheese available in tins, fresh cottage cheese (*paneer*) and mozzarella cheese which is a low fat variety. You could experiment with others but make sure to check with their properties since all of them will not give the required texture once baked.

7. Many ovens have marks instead of temperatures. Please check the oven's user reference manual to understand which mark indicates what temperature, for best results.

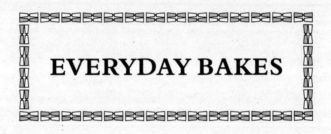

EVERYDAY BAKES

☾ **Baked Pesto Pasta** ☽

Here is a unique and innovative blend of fresh basil, olive oil and pine nuts mixed with cream and tossed with Fusilli and wholesome vegetables. You will fall in love with it! Pesto, a famous Pasta sauce, is used as a baking sauce here.

Preparation time: 25 minutes.   Cooking time: 10 minutes.   Serves 4.
Baking Temperature: 200°C (400°F).   Baking Time: 15 minutes.

2½ cups cooked fusilli pasta, page 93
1 tsp chopped garlic
¼ cup coloured capsicum (red, yellow, green) cubes
½ cup broccoli florets
½ cup sliced mushrooms (*khumbh*)
½ cup white sauce, page 91
2 tbsp fresh cream
2 tbsp milk
3 tsp oil for cooking
Salt and pepper to taste

To be blended together for the pesto sauce
½ cup pinenuts (*chilgoza*) / walnuts (*akhrot*)
2½ cups chopped fresh basil leaves
2 tsp chopped garlic
3 tbsp olive oil
Salt to taste

Other ingredients
¼ cup grated mozzarella cheese
Butter for greasing

1. Heat 1 tsp of oil in a pan, add the garlic and sauté for ½ a minute.
2. Add the fusilli pasta, mix gently and keep aside.
3. Heat the remaining 2 tsp of oil in another pan and add the vegetables and sauté for 5 minutes.
4. Add the salt and pepper, mix well and keep aside.
5. Combine the pasta, white sauce, pesto sauce, sautéed vegetables, cream, milk, salt and pepper. Mix well.
6. Spread the mixture in a greased baking dish.
7. Sprinkle cheese on top and bake in a pre-heated oven at 200°C (400°F) for 10 minutes.
   Serve hot.

Baked Kidney Beans with Alfredo Sauce

The beans are cooked in Mexican chillies con carne style with vegetables in a spicy stew-like dish made with tomatoes, onions and capsicums, spiked with chillies. Stuffed in tortillas and then baked with a sinful cheesy sauce, exciting is one word to describe this dish.

Preparation time: 10 minutes.   Cooking time: 20 minutes.   Serves 4.
Baking Temperature: 200°C (400°F).   Baking Time: 20 minutes.

8 tortillas, page 100

For the kidney beans mixture
1 cup boiled *rajma* (kidney beans)
½ cup onions, cut into quarters
½ cup coloured capsicum (green, yellow, red) cubes
1 tbsp mixed herbs
1 tsp finely chopped green chillies
¼ cup tomato purée
1 tsp Tabasco sauce

14

1½ tbsp oil for cooking
Salt and pepper to taste

For the Alfredo sauce
1 tbsp butter
1 tbsp plain flour (*maida*)
1 cup milk
¼ cup grated cheese
Salt and pepper to taste

Other ingredients
¼ cup grated cheese

For the kidney beans mixture
1. Heat the oil in a pan, add the onions, capsicums, mixed herbs, green chillies, mix well and sauté on medium flame for 10 minutes till they become soft.
2. Add the tomato purée, ½ cup water and salt, cover the pan with a lid and cook for 5 minutes stirring once in between till the mixture thickens.
3. Add the *rajma*, Tabasco sauce and pepper and cook for another 5 minutes on low flame.
4. Divide the mixture into 8 equal portions. Keep aside

For the Alfredao sauce
1. Heat the butter in a pan, add the flour and cook on a low flame while stirring throughout, until froth appears.
2. Add the milk gradually and stir continuously until the sauce thickens.
3. Add the cheese, salt and pepper and mix well. Keep aside.

How to proceed
1. Place one tortilla on a baking tray, spread 1 portion of the kidney beans mixture and 2 tbsp of the Alfredo sauce.
2. Place another tortilla sheet on top and repeat the above procedure with the remaining 6 tortillas, kidney beans mixture and Alfredo sauce.
3. Sprinkle cheese on top and bake in a pre-heated oven at 200°C (400°F) for 15 minutes.
   Serve hot.

Spinach Gnocchi with Marinara Sauce

Picture on page 19.

Celebrate, Italian-style! Gnocchi are Italian dumplings, which are made of spinach, potato and flour. They can either be poached or steamed. These dumplings are made on special occasions or festivals in Italy. Marinara is a chunky tomato sauce cooked with oregano.
Put both together, and it is indeed a festive meal!

Preparation time: 25 minutes.   Cooking time: 20 minutes.   Serves 4.
Baking Temperature: 150°C (300°F).   Baking Time: 15 minutes.

For the gnocchi
2 cups mashed potatoes
¾ cup blanched and chopped spinach (*palak*)
¼ cup plain flour (*maida*)
¼ tsp baking powder
1 tbsp oil
1 tsp salt for boiling
Salt and pepper to taste

For the Marinara sauce
1½ cups tomatoes, cut into chunks
2 tbsp butter
2 tsp finely chopped garlic
2 tsp cream
2 tsp oregano
Salt and pepper to taste

Other ingredients
¼ cup grated mozzarella cheese
Butter for greasing

For the gnocchi
1. Combine the potatoes, spinach, plain flour, baking powder, salt and pepper in a bowl to make soft dough.
2. Divide the dough into approximately 35 to 40 equal sized balls.
3. Flatten, each ball gently using a fork.
4. Boil plenty of water in a pan and add 1 tsp of salt and 1 tbsp of oil to the water.

SPINACH GNOCCHI WITH MARINARA SAUCE : Recipe on page 17. ➔

5. When the water boils, add a few pieces of the gnocchi at a time and allow them to half cook for 3 to 4 minutes.
6. Carefully remove the gnocchi from the boiling water, using a perforated spoon. Keep aside.
7. Repeat the same procedure for the remaining gnocchi.

For the Marinara sauce
1. Heat the butter in a pan, add the garlic and sauté for 1 minute.
2. Add the tomato chunks and cook for 2 to 3 minutes till they are soft. If necessary add 2 tbsp of water.
3. Add the cream, oregano, salt and pepper and sauté for another 1 minute. Remove from the flame and keep aside.

How to proceed
1. Layer the gnocchi in a greased rectangular baking dish and pour the marinara sauce on top.
2. Sprinkle cheese on top and bake in a pre-heated oven at 150°C (300°F) for 10 minutes.
   Serve hot.

☾ **Peppery Mushroom and Potato Bake** ☽

A rich mushroom-flavoured bake with layers of potato, this dish features such a perfect blend of flavours that it leaves you reluctant to lay your fork and knife down!

Preparation time: 10 minutes.   Cooking time: 10 minutes.   Serves 4.
Baking Temperature: 200°C (400°F).   Baking Time: 15 minutes.

6 parboiled potatoes, thickly sliced (¼")
½ tsp freshly ground pepper
½ tsp butter
Salt to taste

For the mushroom sauce
1 cup sliced mushrooms (*khumbh*)
1 tbsp chopped onions
½ tsp finely chopped garlic
½ tsp finely chopped green chillies
½ cup white sauce, page 91
1 tbsp butter
Salt and pepper to taste

Other ingredients
Butter for greasing
¼ cup grated cheese

For the mushroom sauce
1. Heat the butter in a pan, add the onions and sauté till they turn translucent.
2. Add the garlic, green chillies and mushrooms and sauté till the mushrooms become soft.
3. Add ¼ cup of water and cook for 2 to 3 minutes.
4. Add the white sauce, salt and pepper. Mix well and keep aside.

How to proceed
1. Heat the butter in a pan, add the potatoes, salt and pepper. Toss well and keep aside.
2. Place a few potato slices at the bottom of a greased baking dish and pour some mushroom sauce on top.
3. Repeat steps 1 and 2 to make alternate layers of potato slices and mushroom sauce.
4. Sprinkle cheese on top and bake in a pre-heated oven at 200°C (400°F) for 10 minutes.
   Serve hot.

© **Baked Vegetable Risotto** ☽

Rice, which is the first course of an Italian meal, takes on an exciting and wholesome avatar here, loaded with veggies. Risotto is usually made with special kind of rice called Arborio rice, which is extremely absorbent and gives a creamy consistency to the dish even though the grains remain separate. Since Arborio rice is not easily available in India replace it with brown rice which works equally well.

Preparation time: 10 minutes.   Cooking time: 15 minutes.   Serves 4.
Baking Temperature: 200°C (400°F).   Baking Time: 20 minutes.

2½ cups cooked brown rice, page 95
½ cup chopped coloured capsicums (red, yellow, green)
¼ cup chopped onions
¼ cup chopped mushrooms (*khumbh*)
1½ cups milk
3 tbsp cream
2 tbsp white wine (optional)
½ cup grated cheese
2 tbsp butter
Salt and pepper to taste

23

1. Heat the butter in a pan, add the onions and sauté till they turn translucent.
2. Add the capsicums and sauté till they become soft.
3. Add the mushrooms and cook till done.
4. Add the rice, milk, cream and ¼ cup cheese and mix well. Bring to boil and simmer for a few minutes.
5. Add the wine and mix well.
6. Put the mixture in a greased baking dish and sprinkle cheese on top.
7. Bake in a pre-heated oven at 200°C (400°F) for 15 minutes.
   Serve hot.

ℭ **Fusion Bake** ℈

Here is a fabulous casserole bake, flavoured with olives and coated with creamy white sauce and cheese. Cottage cheese adds a crumbly texture to the dish, even as vinegar adds a tangy tinge!

Preparation time: 20 minutes.   Cooking time: Nil.   Serves 4.
Baking Temperature: 200°C (400°F).   Baking Time: 15 to 20 minutes.

2 cups cooked Farfalle pasta (bow shaped), page 93
1 cup crumbled *paneer* (cottage cheese)
½ cup chopped tomatoes
2 tbsp chopped olives
2 tsp vinegar
2 tsp oil
Salt and pepper to taste

To be mixed for the cream sauce
¼ cup curds (*dahi*)
½ cup milk
¼ cup cheese
2 tbsp plain flour *(maida)*

25

Other ingredients
¼ cup grated mozzarella cheese

1. Combine Farfalle pasta, *paneer*, olives, vinegar, oil, tomatoes, salt and pepper in a bowl.
2. Spread the mixture on a greased baking dish.
3. Pour the cream sauce on the mixture.
4. Sprinkle cheese on top and bake in a pre-heated oven at 200°C (400°F) for 10 to 15 minutes.
    Serve hot.

Minty Baked Potatoes

Picture on page 75.

Want to jazz up a lazy Sunday with a tantalising dish for lunch? Try the all-time favourite baked potatoes served with an aromatic mint sauce and sweet corn filling.

Preparation time: 10 minutes.   Cooking time: Nil.   Serves 4.
Baking Temperature: 200°C (400°F).   Baking Time: 30 minutes.

For the baked potatoes
4 large parboiled potatoes
Oil for brushing
Salt to taste

To be mixed into a corn filling
¾ cup boiled American corn
½ cup grated cheese
Salt and pepper to taste

For the mint sauce
½ cup cream
2 tbsp curds (*dahi*)
4 tbsp mint leaves (*phudina*)
Salt and pepper to taste

Other ingredients
¼ cup grated mozzarella cheese

For the baked potatoes
1. Brush the potatoes with oil and sprinkle a little salt over it.

27

2. Wrap in an aluminium foil and bake in a pre-heated oven at 200°C (400°F) for 10 minutes.
3. Cool slightly and cut each baked potato horizontally into two halves.
4. Scoop the potatoes from the insides to make a hollow. Keep aside.

For the mint sauce
1. Beat the cream until thick.
2. Add the curds, mint leaves, salt and pepper and mix well. Keep aside.

How to proceed
1. Fill each potato half with 2 tbsp of the corn filling.
2. Place the potato halves in a greased baking dish and pour 1½ tbsp of the mint sauce on each halve evenly.
3. Sprinkle cheese on top and bake in a pre-heated oven at 200°C (400°F) for 10 minutes.
   Serve hot.

Healthy Variation:

The mint sauce can be made healthy by using ½ cup of Dieter's white sauce, page 92 mixed with 4 tbsp chopped mint leaves.

☾ **Garlic Spaghetti Bake** ☽

A king among spaghetti casseroles, this garlic dominated dish is cooked with tomato sauce, layered with white sauce, and topped with breadcrumbs to give it a crunchy texture.

Preparation time: 20 minutes.   Cooking time: 10 minutes.   Serves 4.
Baking Temperature: 200°C (400°F).   Baking Time: 15 to 20 minutes.

3 cups cooked spaghetti, page 93
¼ cup chopped onions
2 tbsp chopped garlic
1 cup tomato concasse, page 97
½ cup white sauce, page 91
1 tbsp oil for cooking
¼ cup bread crumbs
¼ cup grated mozzarella cheese
Salt and pepper to taste

1. Heat the oil in a pan, add the onions and sauté till they turn translucent.
2. Add the garlic and sauté for ½ minute.

3. Add the tomato concasse, spaghetti, salt and pepper and mix well.
4. Spread the spaghetti mixture at the bottom of a baking dish, pour the white sauce over it and sprinkle bread crumbs on top.
5. Sprinkle cheese on top and bake in a pre-heated oven at 200°C (400°F) for 10 to 15 minutes.

☾ **Asparagus and Corn Augratin** ☽

Asparagus and corn come together augratin; in a delectable dish that is ideal for small family dinners. Augratin typically means 'covered with cheese, filled with white sauce and baked in an oven'. You may be amused to note that the literal translation of the French phrase is 'with the burnt scrapings from the pan'!

Preparation time: 20 minutes.   Cooking time: Nil.   Serves 4.
Baking Temperature: 200°C (400°F).   Baking Time: 15 to 20 minutes.

1 cup boiled sweet corn *(makai/ bhutta)*
1 cup boiled asparagus spears, cut into ½" long pieces
1½ cups white sauce, page 91
½ cup grated mozzarella cheese
Salt and pepper to taste
Butter for greasing

1. Combine the corn, asparagus, white sauce, salt and pepper in a bowl and mix well.
2. Pour this mixture in a greased baking dish.

3. Sprinkle cheese on top and bake in a pre-heated oven at 200°C (400°F) for 10 to 15 minutes or till the cheese melts and is lightly browned.
   Serve hot.

Healthy Variation:

Substitute white sauce with Dieter's white sauce, page 92.

Original Lasagne

Picture on cover.

Yes, we are talking about Garfield's favourite dish! Here is a vegetarian variation of the original preparation sans the minced meat, with the authentic white and red sauces and loaded with cheese. Lasagne sheets are available in a standard size in the market, so portioning is not a problem.

Preparation time: 25 minutes.   Cooking time: Nil.   Serves 4.
Baking Temperature: 200°C (400°F).   Baking Time: 30 minutes.

6 cooked lasagne sheets, page 93
¾ cup white sauce, page 91
¾ cup basic tomato sauce, page 98
¼ cup grated cheese
Butter for greasing

1. Divide the white sauce and basic tomato sauce into 3 equal portions.
2. Place one lasagne sheet on the bottom of an 200 mm. (8") diameter greased baking dish.

3. Spread 1 portion of the white sauce over the sheet and place another lasagne sheet on it.
4. Spread 1 portion of tomato sauce and place another lasagne sheet on it.
5. Repeat the same procedure with the remaining lasagne sheets, tomato sauce and white sauce. Finish off with the tomato sauce as the last layer.
6. Sprinkle cheese on top and bake in a pre-heated oven at 200°C (400°F) for 25 minutes.
   Serve hot.

Healthy Variations:

1. Replace Lasagne sheets with whole wheat rotis.
2. Use Dieter's white sauce, page 92 instead of white sauce.
3. Lasagne can be topped with mozzarella cheese.

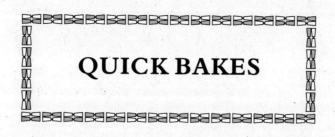

QUICK BAKES

Baked Mushroom Macaroni

Picture on facing page.

Macaroni fits well into almost any baked dish. Here's a quick combo of macaroni and vegetables, which satiates your hunger pangs and delights your taste buds at the same time.

Preparation time: 10 minutes. Cooking time: 7 minutes. Serves 4.
Baking Temperature: 200°C (400°F). Baking Time: 15 minutes.

2 cups cooked macaroni, page 93

For the vegetable layer
½ cup chopped onions
1 cup chopped coloured capsicums (red and yellow)
1 cup chopped tomatoes
1 cup sliced mushrooms (*khumbh*)
2 tbsp oregano
2 tbsp sliced olives
2 tbsp butter
Salt and pepper to taste

BAKED MUSHROOM MACARONI : Recipe above. →

To be mixed into a mushroom sauce
¼ cup readymade mushroom soup powder
1½ cups water

Other ingredients
¼ cup grated mozzarella cheese
Butter for greasing
Few sliced black olives to serve

For the vegetable layer
1. Heat the butter in a pan, add the onions and sauté till they turn translucent.
2. Add the capsicum, tomatoes and mushrooms and sauté for another 2 minutes.
3. Add the oregano, olives, salt, pepper and mix well. Keep aside.

How to proceed
1. Arrange the macaroni on the bottom of a greased baking dish.
2. Spread the vegetable layer on top of the pasta and pour the mushroom sauce on top.
3. Sprinkle cheese on top and bake in a pre-heated oven at 200°C (400°F) for 10 minutes.
4. Top with olives and serve hot.

☾ **Zucchini and Brinjal Bake** ☽

Zucchini and brinjals sautéed with garlic and layered with a tangy tomato sauce, this delectable baked dish acquires a velvety appearance as it is topped with cheese.

Preparation time: 10 minutes.   Cooking time: 25 minutes.   Serves 4.
Baking Temperature: 200°C (400°F).   Baking Time: 15 minutes.

For the filling
2 cups sliced zucchini
2 cups sliced brinjal (*baingan* / eggplant)
4 tsp finely chopped garlic
4 tsp oil
Salt to taste

To be mixed into a tomato sauce
4 tbsp readymade tomato soup powder
2 cups water

Other ingredients
¼ cup grated mozzarella cheese

For the filling
1. Heat 2 tsp of oil in a pan, add 2 tsp of garlic and sauté for ½ a minute.
2. Add the zucchini and salt and sauté till half done. Remove and keep aside.
3. Heat the remaining 2 tsp oil in the same pan, add the remaining 2 tsp garlic and sauté for ½ minute.
4. Add the brinjal and salt and sauté till half done. Remove and keep aside.

How to proceed
1. Arrange the zucchini on the bottom of a greased baking dish and pour half the sauce on top.
2. Arrange the brinjal as a second layer and pour the remaining tomato sauce on it.
3. Sprinkle cheese on top and bake in a pre-heated oven at 200°C (400°F) for 10 minutes.
   Serve hot.

Fettuccine Spinach Bake

Think of greens and cottage cheese, and Palak Paneer might be the first dish that comes to your mind! Here is a dish to dispel that thought. Spinach and cottage cheese blended together and flavoured with a dash of nutmeg, this baked dish shall surely win over your heart!

Preparation time: 15 minutes.   Cooking time: 5 minutes.   Serves 4.
Baking Temperature: 200°C (400°F).   Baking Time: 15 minutes.

2 cups cooked fettuccine pasta, page 93
¼ cup grated mozzarella cheese

For the spinach mixture
1½ cups blanched and chopped spinach (*palak*)
¼ cup finely chopped onions
2 tsp finely chopped garlic
1 tbsp oil
Salt and pepper to taste

To be blended into a smooth *paneer* sauce
1 cup grated *paneer* (cottage cheese)

41

¾ cup milk
1 tsp ground nutmeg (*jaiphal*) powder
1 tsp black pepper powder
Salt to taste

For the spinach mixture
1. Heat the oil in a pan, add the onions and garlic and sauté till they turn translucent.
2. Add the spinach, salt and pepper and sauté for another 2 minutes. Keep aside.

How to proceed
1. Combine the *paneer* sauce, fettuccine and the spinach mixture in a bowl. Mix well till the sauce coats the fettuccine evenly.
2. Spread the mixture in a rectangular baking dish.
3. Sprinkle cheese on top and bake in a pre-heated oven at 200°C (400°F) for 10 minutes.
   Serve hot.

Healthy Variation:

Use low fat *paneer*, page 102, instead of regular *paneer*.

Baked Noodles with Spinach and Yoghurt

An unusual combination of noodles and curds, all mixed together and baked, this is one quick, easy and tasty dish to conjure up. The dish is usually a little sour, but if you like it otherwise then add a pinch of sugar.

Preparation time: 10 minutes.   Cooking time: 5 minutes.   Serves 4.
Baking Temperature: 200°C (400°F).   Baking Time: 25 minutes.

2½ cups cooked spaghetti, page 93
2 cups blanched and chopped spinach (*palak*)
½ cup finely chopped onions
½ cup hung curds (*dahi*)
¾ cup grated processed cheese
¼ cup plain flour (*maida*)
2 tsp oil
Salt and pepper to taste

1. Heat the oil in a pan, add the onions and sauté till they turn translucent. Keep aside.
2. Combine spaghetti, spinach, onions, curds, cheese, plain flour, salt and pepper in a bowl. Mix well.
3. Layer the mixture in a baking dish.
4. Sprinkle cheese on top and bake in a pre-heated oven at 200°C (400°F) for 20 minutes.
   Serve hot.

Handy tip: Approximately 2 cups fresh curds will yield 1 cup of hung curds when hung in muslin cloth for 20 minutes.

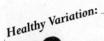

Use 2 cups boiled vegetables or rice noodles instead of spaghetti.

Vegetable Augratin

Loaded with cheese and the goodness of vegetables, this simple and tasty dish is so famous that it has become almost synonymous with the term 'baked dish'!

Preparation time: 20 minutes.   Cooking time: Nil.   Serves 4.
Baking Temperature: 200°C (400°F).   Baking Time: 15 to 20 minutes.

2 cups chopped mixed boiled vegetables (carrots, peas, french beans),
½ cup white sauce, page 91
½ cup grated mozzarella cheese
Salt and pepper to taste

1. Combine the vegetables, white sauce, salt and pepper in a bowl and mix well.
2. Spread the mixture in a baking dish.
3. Sprinkle cheese on top and bake in a pre-heated oven at 200°C (400°F) for 10 to 15 minutes or till the cheese melts and is lightly browned.
    Serve hot.

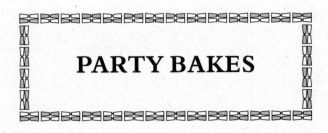

PARTY BAKES

☾ **Spinach Malfati** ☾

Here is a famous Italian dish, which does not really qualify as a baked dish because it is baked only to melt the cheese, but an interesting recipe nonetheless. Even a mere thought of these steamed dumplings, topped with tomato gravy and dotted with cheese, is no less than scintillating!

Preparation time: 15 minutes.   Cooking time: 20 minutes.   Serves 4.
Baking Temperature: 200°C (400°F).   Baking Time: 15 minutes.

For the spinach dumplings
3 cups finely chopped spinach (*palak*)
¾ cup crumbled *paneer* (cottage cheese)
2 pinches nutmeg (*jaiphal*) powder
½ tsp chopped green chillies
2 tbsp plain flour (*maida*)
2 pinches baking powder
Salt to taste

For the tomato gravy
1½ cups tomato concasse, page 97

47

1 tbsp chopped garlic
¼ cup chopped spring onion whites
1 tbsp red chilli flakes *(paprika)*
2 tbsp tomato purée
4 tbsp cream
2 tbsp oil
Salt to taste

For the topping
¼ cup grated cheese

For the spinach dumplings
1. Steam the spinach for 5 minutes and squeeze out the water. Keep aisde for use in the tomato sauce.
2. Mix all the ingredients and shape into 15 to 20 small balls.
3. Steam for 5 minutes. Keep aside.

For the tomato gravy
1. Heat the oil in a pan, add the garlic and spring onion whites and sauté for 1 minute.
2. Add the tomato concasse and cook till the sauce thickens.

3. Add the red chilli flakes, tomato purée, salt and ½ cup of water and bring to a boil.
4. Add the cream, mix well and keep aside.

How to proceed
1. Place the dumplings in a baking dish.
2. Pour the tomato gravy on them and sprinkle cheese on top.
3. Bake in a pre-heated oven at 200°C (400°F) for 10 minutes.
   Serve hot.

Healthy Variations:

1. To make the tomato gravy, instead of cream use low fat cream or a mixture of ¼ cup low fat milk mixed with 1 tsp cornflour and cook the sauce till it thickens.
2. Regular *paneer* can be substituted with low fat *paneer*, page 102.

☾ **Tortilla Bake** ☽

This layered tortilla casserole is stuffed with cottage cheese and a rich, thick and creamy mustard-flavoured sauce that adds a pungent flavour to the dish. Truly a party fare!

Preparation time: 20 minutes.   Cooking time: 7 minutes.   Serves 4.
Baking Temperature: 200°C (400°F).   Baking Time: 15 to 20 minutes.

6 tortillas, page 100

For the filling
½ cup grated *paneer* (cottage cheese)
¼ cup chopped onions
1 cup chopped tomatoes
½ tbsp tomato ketchup
½ tsp chilli powder
2 tbsp oil for cooking
Salt and pepper to taste

To be mixed together for the mustard sauce
½ cup grated cheese
1 tsp red chilli flakes (*paprika*)
2 tbsp cream
2 tbsp thick curds (*dahi*)
1 tsp butter
1 tsp prepared mustard paste
Salt and pepper to taste

Other ingredients
¼ cup grated cheese
Butter for greasing

For the filling
1. Heat the oil in a pan, add the onions and sauté till they turn translucent.
2. Add the tomatoes and cook for 2 to 3 minutes.
3. Add the tomato ketchup, chilli powder, *paneer*, salt and pepper and mix well. Keep aside.
4. Divide the filling into 4 equal portions. Keep aside.

How to proceed
1. Place one tortilla at the bottom of a 200 mm. (8") diameter greased baking dish.
2. Spread 1 portion of the filling over the tortilla and place another tortilla on it.
3. Spread 2 tbsp of mustard sauce and place another tortilla on it.
4. Repeat the same procedure with the remaining tortillas, filling and mustard sauce. Finish off with the filling as the last layer.
5. Sprinkle cheese on top and bake in a pre-heated oven at 200°C (400°F) for 10 to 15 minutes.
   Serve hot.

Healthy Variation:

You could use *chappatis* or Healthy Tortillas, page 101 instead of tortillas.

☾ **Baked Pasta Shells** ☽

Picture on page 55.

Large pasta shells filled with spinach and cottage cheese and topped with tangy tomato sauce, it is no wonder that children love this dish! A typical party fare, this dish is as good as a delicious and wholesome meal in itself.

Preparation time: 25 minutes.   Cooking time: Nil.   Serves 4.
Baking Temperature: 200°C (400°F).   Baking Time: 15 minutes.

12 cooked large shell pasta, page 93
1½ cups basic tomato sauce, page 98
Salt and pepper to taste

To be combined into a filling
1 cup grated *paneer* (cottage cheese)
1 cup blanched and chopped spinach (*palak*)
Salt and pepper to taste

Other ingredients
¼ cup grated mozzarella cheese
Butter for greasing

1. Place each shell pasta on a 200 mm. (8") diameter greased baking dish.
2. Fill each shell pasta with 2 tbsp of the filling.
3. Pour the tomato sauce on top of the shell pastas evenly.
4. Sprinkle cheese on top and bake in a pre-heated oven at 200°C (400°F) for 10 minutes.
   Serve hot.

BAKED PASTA SHELLS : Recipe on page 53. ↪

Baked Crêpes with Capsicum Sauce

The flavour of savoury crepes stuffed with tangy flavoured cottage cheese is further enhanced by the rich and creamy capsicum sauce. No one can eat just one!

Preparation time: 15 minutes.   Cooking time: 20 minutes.   Serves 4.
Baking Temperature: 200°C (400°F).   Baking Time: 15 minutes.

For the crêpes
¼ cup plain flour *(maida)*
¼ cup cornflour
¼ cup milk
1 tsp melted butter for greasing
A pinch of salt

For the filling
¾ cup crumbled *paneer* (cottage cheese)
1 tsp finely chopped green chillies
¼ cup chopped red capsicum
1 tsp oil
Tabasco sauce to taste

Salt and pepper to taste

For the capsicum sauce
1 large green capsicum, cut into half
1 cup milk
1 tbsp butter
1 tbsp plain flour *(maida)*
Salt and pepper to taste

Other ingredients
¼ cup grated cheese
Butter for greasing

56

For the garnish
2 olives, thinly sliced

For the crêpes
1. Mix the plain flour, cornflour, milk, salt and ½ cup of water. Mix very well until no lumps remain.
2. Grease a 125 mm. (5") diameter non-stick pan with the butter.
3. Pour 2 tbsp of the batter, tilt the pan around quickly so that the batter coats the pan evenly.
4. When the sides starts to peel off, upturn the pancake and cook the other side for 30 seconds.
5. Repeat with the remaining batter to make 5 more pancakes, greasing the pan with butter when required.

For the filling
1. Heat the oil in a pan, add the green chillies and sauté for ½ a minute.
2. Add the red capsicum and sauté till it turns soft.
3. Add the *paneer*, Tabasco sauce, salt and pepper and mix well. Keep aside.

For the capsicum sauce
1. Boil 2 cups of water, add the capsicum. Boil for 5 minutes, drain and blend with milk in a mixer.
2. Heat the butter in a pan, add the plain flour and sauté for ½ minute.
3. Add the blended capsicum, mix well and keep stirring until the sauce thickens.
4. Add the salt and pepper and mix well. Keep aside.

How to proceed
1. Place 2 tbsp of filling on each crepe and tightly roll up into a long roll.
2. Place the crêpes in a greased baking dish and pour the capsicum sauce on them.
3. Sprinkle cheese on top and bake in a pre-heated oven at 200°C (400°F) for 10 minutes. Serve hot garnished with olives.

Handy Tip: Pancakes can be made ahead of time and stored in plastic film in the fridge.

Healthy Variations:

1. Use healthy tortillas, page 101, instead of crêpes.
2. The capsicum sauce can be made by using low fat milk and substituting plain flour with whole wheat flour.

58

◠ Spicy Mexican Pasta Bake ◡

As good as a visit to Mexico! Try this delicious Mexican vegetable pasta bake, which is topped with the all-time favourite Mexican salsa sauce and loaded with cheese, which adds a smooth texture to the dish. The coriander and cumin flavoured white sauce adds more zing to this dish!

Preparation time: 20 minutes.   Cooking time: 10 minutes.   Serves 4.
Baking Temperature: 200°C (400°F).   Baking Time: 15 to 20 minutes.

2 cups cooked penne pasta, page 93
¼ cup chopped onions
¼ cup chopped coloured capsicums (red and yellow)
2 tsp cumin seeds (*jeera*) powder
2 tsp red chilli flakes (*paprika*)
1½ cups white sauce, page 91
2 tbsp chopped coriander (*dhania*)
1 tbsp oil
Salt and pepper to taste

For the salsa sauce
1 cup chopped tomatoes

¼ cup chopped onions
¼ cup chopped green capsicum
1 tsp chilli powder
2 tsp oil
Salt and pepper to taste

Other ingredients
¼ cup grated cheese
Butter for greasing

For the salsa sauce
1. Heat the oil in a pan, add the onions and sauté till they turn translucent.
2. Add the capsicum and sauté till they become soft.
3. Add the tomatoes, chilli powder, salt and pepper and mix well. Keep aside.

How to proceed
1. Heat the oil in a pan, add the onions and sauté till they turn translucent.
2. Add the coloured capsicums, cumin seeds powder and red chilli flakes and sauté for 2 minutes.
3. Add the pasta, white sauce, coriander, salt and pepper and mix well.
4. Spread the pasta evenly in a greased baking dish.
5. Pour the salsa sauce on top of the pasta.
6. Sprinkle cheese on top and bake in a pre-heated oven at 200°C (400°F) for 10 to 15 minutes.
   Serve hot.

Healthy Variations:
1. Pasta can be substituted with 2 cups of whole wheat pasta or 2 cups of boiled vegetables like corn, carrots and capsicum.
2. Use Dieter's white sauce, page 92, instead of white sauce.

☾ **Pomodoro Lasagne** ☽

This elegant vegetable lasagne showcases the merits of both tomato and cream sauce. The rich baked dish is packed with layers of pasta filled with vegetables and tomatoes topped with Italian mozzarella cheese and baked until golden brown in colour. Pomodoro sauce, that is, tomato sauce flavoured with basil, adds a unique flavour to this dish.

Preparation time: 15 minutes.   Cooking time: 10 minutes.   Serves 4.
Baking Temperature: 200°C (400°F).   Baking Time: 20 minutes.

6 cooked lasagne sheets, page 93

For the Pomodoro sauce
1 cup tomato concasse, page 97
½ cup finely chopped onions
1 tsp finely chopped garlic
¼ cup chopped fresh basil leaves
2 tsp cream
3 tsp olive oil
Salt to taste

For the vegetable mixture
½ cup blanched broccoli florets
½ cup sliced mushrooms (*khumbh*)
½ cup boiled American corn
½ cup chopped capsicum
2 tbsp oil for cooking

To be mixed for the cream sauce
½ cup fresh cream
Salt and pepper to taste

Other ingredients
¼ cup grated cheese
Butter for greasing

For the Pomodoro sauce
1. Heat the oil in a pan, add the onions and garlic sauté for 3 to 4 minutes.
2. Add the tomato concasse, basil leaves, salt and sauté for 4 to 5 minutes.
3. Add the cream and mix well.
4. Divide the sauce into 3 equal portions and keep aside.

For the vegetable mixture
1. Heat the oil in a pan, add the capsicum and sauté for ½ a minute.
2. Add the remaining vegetables and sauté till the vegetables become dry.
3. Add the salt and pepper and mix well.
4. Divide the mixture into 3 equal portions and keep aside.

How to proceed

1. Place one lasagne sheet on the bottom of a 200 mm. (8") diameter greased baking dish.
2. Spread 1 portion of the vegetables over the sheet. Pour 2 tbsp of cream sauce and place another lasagne sheet on it.
3. Spread 1 portion of Pomodoro sauce and place another lasagne sheet on it.
4. Repeat the same procedure with the remaining lasagne sheets, vegetable mixture, Pomodoro sauce and cream sauce.
5. Sprinkle cheese on top and bake in a pre-heated oven at 200°C (400°F) for 15 minutes.
   Serve hot.

Healthy Variation:

Use low fat cream locally available in the market instead of cream.

☾ **Stuffed Bulgur and Brinjal Bake** ☽

Picture on facing page.

*Brinjals are filled with spicy cracked wheat, which is cooked with assorted vegetables and
mixed with rich creamy tomato sauce. You will fall head-over-heels in love
with this scrumptious dish!*

Preparation time: 10 minutes.   Cooking time: 25 minutes.   Serves 4.
Baking Temperature: 200°C (400°F).   Baking Time: 15 minutes.

2 big brinjal (*baingan* / eggplant)

For the mixture
1 cup bulgur wheat (*dalia*)
¼ cup chopped onions
2 tsp chopped garlic
¼ cup chopped carrots
¼ cup deseeded and diced tomatoes
¼ cup chopped capsicum

STUFFED BULGUR AND BRINJAL BAKE : Recipe above. ↪

½ cup chopped mushrooms (*khumbh*)
1 tsp chilli powder
1 tbsp chopped coriander (*dhania*)
2 tsp oregano
1 tbsp cream
1 tbsp oil
Salt and pepper to taste

To be mixed for the tomato sauce (for the mixture)
2 tbsp readymade tomato soup powder
⅓ cup water

Other ingredients
¼ cup grated cheese
Butter for greasing

For the mixture
1. Boil 1½ cups of water in a pan, add the bulgur wheat and cook till it softens. Drain and keep aside.
2. Heat the oil in another pan, add the onions and garlic and sauté till the onions turn translucent.
3. Add the carrots, capsicum, mushrooms, tomatoes, chilli powder, coriander and sauté for another few minutes till they are cooked.

4. Add the bulgur wheat, oregano, salt and pepper stir for another 1 minute.
5. Add the prepared tomato sauce and cream, mix well and cook for 2 more minutes.
6. Divide the mixture into 4 equal portions and keep aside.

How to proceed
1. Boil water in a pan, cut the brinjal into two halves and place them in boiling water and cook till soft.
2. Remove and cool.
3. Scoop the flesh of the brinjal and discard it.
4. Stuff each half of the brinjal with 1 portion of the mixture and place them in greased baking dish.
5. Repeat the same procedure for the other brinjal.
6. Sprinkle the cheese on top and bake in a pre-heated oven at 200°C (400°F) for 10 minutes.
   Serve hot.

Healthy Variation:

You can avoid the cheese and instead top with little of the prepared tomato sauce.

c **Baked Stuffed Capsicum** ɔ

Capsicums with a rich and creamy risotto filling and gratinated with cheese, this is a wholesome and tasty dish that is sure to captivate you!

Preparation time: 10 minutes.   Cooking time: 10 minutes.   Serves 4.
Baking Temperature: 200°C (400°F).   Baking Time: 15 minutes.

4 red capsicums, cut into halves and deseeded

For the risotto filling
1½ cups cooked brown rice, page 95
2 tsp finely chopped garlic
3 tbsp chopped celery
¾ cup milk
3 tbsp cream
¼ cup grated cheese
2 tbsp butter
Salt and freshly crushed pepper to taste

Other ingredients
½ cup grated mozzarella cheese

For the risotto filling
1. Heat the butter in a pan, add the garlic and celery and sauté for a few seconds.
2. Add the brown rice, milk, cream and cheese and mix well. Bring to a boil and simmer for a few minutes, adding a little water if required.
3. Add the salt and pepper and mix well. Keep aside.

How to proceed
1. Stuff each capsicum half with ¼ cup of the filling and place in a greased baking dish.
2. Sprinkle cheese on top and bake in a pre-heated oven at 200°C (400°F) for 10 minutes.
   Serve hot.

Baked Cannelloni with Pomodoro Sauce

The word cannelloni is derived from "canna" and literally means big tubes of pasta. Filled with mixed vegetables and cottage cheese, the cannelloni when coated with Pomodoro sauce, evolves into a dish that you just cannot resist gobbling up!

Preparation time: 20 minutes.   Cooking time: 5 minutes.   Serves 4.
Baking Temperature: 200°C (400°F).   Baking Time: 15 minutes.

8 cooked cannelloni, page 93
1 recipe Pomodoro sauce, page 61

For the stuffing
1 cup finely chopped mixed boiled vegetables (carrots, french beans, cauliflower, green peas)
½ cup *paneer* (cottage cheese)
¼ cup chopped onions
1 tsp chilli powder
2 tsp oil

Salt to taste

Other ingredients
¼ cup grated mozzarella cheese
Butter for greasing

For the stuffing
1. Heat the oil in a pan, add the onions and sauté till they turn translucent.
2. Add the remaining ingredients and cook for 2 minutes.
3. Divide the stuffing into 8 equal portions and keep aside.

How to proceed
1. Fill each cannelloni with 1 portion of the stuffing.
2. Arrange all the cannelloni on a greased baking dish and pour Pomodoro sauce on top.
3. Sprinkle cheese on top and bake in a pre-heated oven at 200°C (400°F) for 10 minutes.
   Serve hot.

Baked Spaghetti with Cheese Balls in Spinach Sauce

Yummy cheese balls baked with a creamy spinach sauce, this dish has an exquisite and sumptuous nature that lures every food lover.

Preparation time: 20 minutes.   Cooking time: 15 minutes.   Serves 4.
Baking Temperature: 200°C (400°F).   Baking Time: 20 to 25 minutes.

For the spaghetti
1½ cups cooked spaghetti, page 93
¼ cup chopped onions
1½ tsp finely chopped green chillies
1 tbsp butter
Salt to taste

For the cheese balls
1½ cups *paneer* (cottage cheese)
2 slices bread
3 tbsp fresh curds (*dahi*)

72

1 tbsp chopped coriander (*dhania*)
3 finely chopped green chillies
4 tbsp plain flour (*maida*)
¼ tsp soda bi-carb
Salt to taste

To be blended for the spinach sauce
1 cup blanched and chopped spinach (*palak*)
½ cup fresh cream
1 cup white sauce, page 91
Salt and pepper to taste

Other ingredients
¼ cup grated mozzarella cheese
Oil for deep frying

For the spaghetti
1. Heat the butter in a pan, add the onions and sauté till they turn translucent. Keep aside.
2. Add the green chillies, spaghetti and salt. Mix well and cook for ½ minute.

For the cheese balls
1. Soak the bread slices in curds for 10 minutes.
2. Crumble the *paneer* and knead very well.
3. Add the soaked bread slices, coriander, green chillies, plain flour, soda bi-carb and salt.
4. Mix well and shape into small balls.
5. Heat the oil in a pan and deep fry the balls till golden brown.
6. Drain on absorbent paper and keep aside.

How to proceed
1. Combine the spaghetti with the spinach sauce and mix well.
2. Spread the mixture on a greased baking dish and arrange the cheese balls on top.
3. Sprinkle the cheese on top and bake in a pre-heated oven at 200°C (400°F) for 15 to 20 minutes.
   Serve hot.

MINTY BAKED POTATOES : Recipe on page 27. ➜

Fresh Corn Enchiladas

An adaptation of the famous Mexican dish, here the tortillas are roasted and stuffed with corn and cottage cheese, topped with Mexican tomato sauce and finally baked to make a delicious meal that will make you the most popular host/hostess.

Preparation time: 20 minutes.   Cooking time: 20 minutes.   Serves 4.
Baking Temperature: 200°C (400°F).   Baking Time: 20 minutes.

4 tortillas, page 100

For the Mexican tomato sauce
1 cup tomato concasse, page 97
¼ cup chopped onions
1 tsp chopped green chillies
½ tsp chilli powder
¼ tsp oregano
2 pinches sugar
2 tbsp oil

Salt to taste

To be mixed into a stuffing
¾ cup cooked sweet corn (*makai/ bhutta*)
½ cup grated *paneer* (cottage cheese)
1 tsp finely chopped green chillies
1 tbsp chopped coriander (*dhania*)
¼ cup chopped deseeded tomatoes
Salt to taste

Other ingredients
¼ cup grated cheese
Butter for greasing

For the Mexican tomato sauce
1. Heat the oil in a pan, add the onions and sauté till they turn translucent. Add the green chillies and sauté for a few seconds.
2. Add the tomatoes, chilli powder, oregano, sugar and salt. Mix well and cook for 5 minutes. Keep aside.

How to proceed

1. Pour 1/3 of the Mexican tomato sauce at the bottom of a greased baking dish.
2. Divide the stuffing into 4 equal portions.
3. Place 1 portion of stuffing on each tortilla and roll up tightly.
4. Arrange each tortilla in the baking dish with the seam facing downwards. Moisten the tops of the tortillas evenly with the remaining Mexican tomato sauce.
5. Sprinkle the cheese over the enchiladas and bake in a pre-heated oven at 200°C (400°F) for 15 minutes.
   Serve hot.

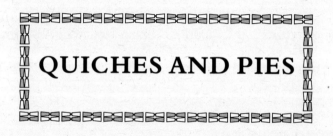

QUICHES AND PIES

ℂ **Spinach and Corn Quiche** ℑ

The pastry base is filled with a cheesy white sauce mixed with blanched spinach and American corn to give an attractive colour and flavour to the dish. Try it once and it is sure to become a hot favourite!

Preparation time: 10 minutes.   Cooking time: 15 minutes.   Makes 1 quiche (6").
Baking Temperature: 200°C (400°F).   Baking Time: 12 to 15 minutes.

1 recipe short crust pastry, page 96
¼ cup grated mozzarella cheese

For the spinach and corn mixture
2 cups shredded spinach (*palak*)
¾ cup boiled American corn (*makai / bhutta*)
1 tbsp butter

For the cheesy white sauce
2 tbsp chopped onions
½ tsp chopped green chillies
1 tbsp plain flour (*maida*)

80

1 cup milk
½ cup grated cheese
2 tbsp butter
Salt and pepper to taste

For the spinach and corn mixture
1. Heat the butter in a pan, add the spinach and sauté till it wilts.
2. Add the corn and sauté for 1 minute. Keep aside.

For the cheesy white sauce
1. Heat the butter in a pan, add the onions and green chillies sauté till they turn translucent.
2. Add the flour and cook on a slow flame, while stirring throughout, until froth appears.
3. Add the milk gradually and stir continuously until the sauce thickens.
4. Add cheese, salt and pepper and mix well.

How to proceed
1. Combine the spinach and corn mixture with the white sauce in a bowl.
2. Spread the mixture over the short crust pastry.
3. Sprinkle cheese on top and bake in a pre-heated oven at 200°C (400°F) for 7 to 10 minutes or till the cheese melts. Cut into 4 wedges and serve hot.

❀ **Baby Corn and Yoghurt Quiche** ❀

*Baby corn and curds make a tangy pie, which apart from being mouth-watering,
also makes for a wholesome meal.*

Preparation time: 20 minutes.   Cooking time: Nil.   Makes 1 quiche (6").
Baking Temperature: 200°C (400°F).   Baking Time: 15 to 20 minutes.

1 recipe short crust pastry, page 96
½ cup boiled baby corn
¼ cup grated cheese

To be mixed into a filling
¾ cup hung curds (*dahi*)
3 tbsp plain flour (*maida*)
A pinch sugar
Few drops of Tabasco sauce
Salt and pepper to taste

1. Spread the filling evenly over the short crust pastry.
2. Layer the baby corn over the filling and top with the cheese.
3. Bake in a pre-heated oven at 200°C (400°F) for 10 to 15 minutes. Cut into 4 equal wedges and serve hot.

Mediterranean Vegetable Pie

Picture on facing page.

A rich tomato pastry base topped with a mouth-watering selection of vegetables and cheese, this delectable dish will excite your taste buds and set your gastronomic juices working in overdrive!

Preparation time: 15 minutes.   Cooking time: 5 minutes.   Makes 1 pie (6").
Baking Temperature: 200°C (400°F).   Baking Time: 15 to 20 minutes.

1 recipe short crust pastry, page 96
¼ cup basic tomato sauce, page 98
¼ cup grated mozzarella cheese

For the topping
½ cup sliced brinjal (*baingan* / eggplant)
½ cup sliced yellow capsicum
¼ cup sundried tomatoes
1 tsp finely chopped garlic
2 tsp oil
Salt and pepper to taste

MEDITERRANEAN VEGETABLE PIE: Recipe above. ↪

For the topping
1. Heat the oil in a pan, add the garlic and sauté for ½ minute.
2. Add the brinjal, yellow capsicum and sundried tomatoes and cook till half done.
3. Add the salt and pepper, mix well and keep aside.

How to proceed
1. Spread the basic tomato sauce over the short crust pastry.
2. Arrange the topping neatly on the crust.
3. Sprinkle cheese on top and bake in a pre-heated oven at 200°C (400°F) for 10 to 15 minutes.
4. Cut into 4 equal wedges and serve hot.

Note: The image shows a deep pie crust which is made by doubling the basic short crust pastry recipe and baking it in a deep loose bottom pie-dish which is approx. 8" wide and 1" to 1½" deep.

☾ **Cauliflower and Broccoli Pie** ☽

What makes this pie extremely attractive is not just its unique taste but also the fact that the case can be made in advance and frozen before being baked. The pastry once baked is then filled with cauliflower and broccoli florets, coated with a creamy white sauce and once again baked to perfection.

Preparation time: 20 minutes.   Cooking time: Nil.   Makes 1 pie (6").
Baking Temperature: 200°C (400°F).   Baking Time: 15 to 20 minutes.

1 recipe short crust pastry, page 96
1 cup boiled cauliflower florets
1 cup blanched broccoli florets

1 cup white sauce, page 91
¼ cup grated mozzarella cheese
Salt and pepper to taste

1. Combine the cauliflower florets, broccoli florets, white sauce, salt and pepper in a bowl and mix well.
2. Fill the mixture in the short crust pastry.
3. Sprinkle cheese on top and bake in a pre-heated oven at 200°C (400°F) for 10 to 15 minutes.
   Cut into 4 equal wedges and serve hot.

☾ **Mushroom Pie** ☽

The deep, earthy flavour of button mushrooms is enhanced with mushroom sauce and mozzarella cheese, to make a delectable pastry dish.

Preparation time: 10 minutes.   Cooking time: 10 minutes.   Makes 1 pie (6″).
Baking Temperature: 200°C (400°F).   Baking Time: 12 to 15 minutes.

1 recipe short crust pastry, page 96
¼ cup grated mozzarella cheese

For the mushroom filling
¾ cup sliced mushrooms (*khumbh*)
2 tbsp chopped onions
½ tsp chopped green chillies
2 tsp butter
Salt to taste

To be mixed to set for the mushroom sauce (for the mushroom filling)
2 tbsp ready mushroom soup powder
½ cup water

For the mushroom filling
1. Heat butter in a pan, add the onions and sauté till they turn translucent.
2. Add the mushrooms and green chillies and sauté for a minute.
3. Add the mushroom sauce, salt, mix well and cook till the mixture thickens.
   Keep aside.

How to proceed
1. Spread the mushroom filling over the short crust pastry.
2. Sprinkle cheese on top and bake in a pre-heated oven at 200°C (400°F) for 7 to 10 minutes till the cheese melts.
   Cut into 4 equal wedges and serve hot.

BASIC RECIPES

⊂ **White Sauce** ⊃

No baked dish is complete without a white sauce. Here's a version of this versatile sauce, which we have tried and perfected. White sauce can be prepared in large quantities and stored in the fridge for up to two weeks.

Preparation time: a few minutes.   Cooking time: 5 minutes.   Makes 1 cup.

1 cup milk
1 tbsp butter
1 tbsp plain flour (*maida*)
Salt and pepper to taste

1. Heat the butter in a pan, add the flour and cook on a slow flame, while stirring throughout, until froth appears.
2. Add the milk gradually and stir continuously until the sauce thickens.
3. Add the salt and pepper and mix well.
   Use as reqired.

☾ **Dieter's White Sauce** ☽

White sauce is almost synonymous with sinfully rich ingredients! Here is a healthier version for our diet-conscious friends. The taste may vary slightly, but this is undoubtedly healthier!

Preparation time: a few minutes.   Cooking time: 10 minutes.   Makes 1 cup.

¾ cup chopped cauliflower or white pumpkin (*doodhi / lauki*)
½ tbsp low fat butter
½ tbsp whole wheat flour (*gehun ka atta*)
½ cup readymade low fat milk (99.9% fat free or double-tonned)
Salt and pepper to taste

1. Boil the cauliflower in ½ cup of water until soft. Blend in a mixer and strain.
2. Heat the butter in a pan, add the flour and cook for ½ minute.
3. Add the milk and cauliflower purée and cook while stirring the mixture continuously until it becomes thick.
4. Add the salt and pepper. Mix well.
   Use as required.

☾ **Cooked Pasta** ☽

Perfectly cooked pasta should be firm to bite and not over-cooked and soggy. This requires a little know-how and care. That is the reason why we have a seperate recipe on how to cook pasta. The recipe works for all types and shapes of pasta though their cooking time may vary as per the shapes. The volume of small pastas will double, but lasagne sheets, noodles and spaghetti will remain the same quantity. It is not advisable to store cooked pasta; always consume it freshly cooked.

Preparation time: Nil.   Cooking time: 5 to 15 minutes.   Makes 3 cups.

2 cups dried pasta (penne, fusilli, fettuccine, macaroni, farfalle) or sheets of lasagne or spaghetti
2 tbsp oil
1 tsp salt

1. Boil plenty of water in a large pan, add salt and 1 tbsp of oil.
2. Add the dried pasta to the boiling water. For lasagne add one sheet at a time.

3. Cook uncovered, stirring occasionally and gently until the pasta is almost done. Cooking times may vary with the size and the thickness of the pasta. Very small pasta (like macaroni, fusilli, penne) may cook in 5 to 7 minutes, while larger shaped pasta will take 8 to 10 minutes.
4. Immediately drain the cooked pasta into a sieve or a colander. Transfer to a bowl of cold water to refresh it. Drain again and keep aside.
5. Toss the pasta in 1 tbsp of oil as this prevents the pasta from sticking to each other. Use as required.

Cooked Brown Rice

Brown rice is healthier than white rice. In this book I have used it to make Risotto as it imparts an interesting texture akin to Italian Arborio rice.

Preparation time: 10 minutes.   Cooking time: 20 minutes.   Makes 2 cups.

1 cup brown rice
½ tsp oil
Salt to taste

1. Pick, wash and drain the rice. Keep aside.
2. Heat the oil in a pan, add the rice, salt and 3 cups of hot water.
3. Cover and cook over a slow flame till the rice is cooked.
   Use as required.

Short Crust Pastry

This crust is the base for most pastry and pie recipes. The crust is first baked and then the filling is added to make various pies. While making crusts, take care not to knead the dough too much as the crumbly texture will be lost and you will end up with a bread-like texture.

Preparation time: 10 minutes.   Cooking time: Nil.   Makes 1 pastry (6").
Baking Temperature: 200°C (400°F).   Baking Time: 15 minutes.

¾ cup plain flour (*maida*)
¼ cup butter
2 pinches salt

1. Sieve the flour. Add the butter and salt and rub in with your fingertips.
2. Add about 1 tbsp of ice-cold water to make a dough
3. Roll out the dough to about 3 mm. thickness.
4. Arrange the rolled out dough in a 150 mm. (6") diameter pie dish.
5. Press the dough into pie dish and prick with a fork on the bottom and sides.
6. Bake in a pre-heated oven at 200°C (400°F) for 8 to 10 minutes.
7. Do not remove from the pie dish. Use as required.

Note: Use the crust with the pie dish on as the crust needs to be baked again after putting the topping.

Tomato Concasse

This recipe, which is more like a home-made tomato purée, is handy not just to make sauces but also for gravies or fillings.

Preparation time: Nil. Cooking time: 10 minutes. Makes 1 cup (approx.).

6 medium sized tomatoes

1. Bring water to a boil a large vessel.
2. Scoop out and discard the eyes of the tomatoes using the tip of the sharp knife.
3. Make a criss-cross cuts at the base of each tomato.
4. Put the tomatoes in boiling water for 3 to 4 minutes.
5. Remove and put in cold water for some time.
6. When the tomatoes are cool, peel and discard the skin.
7. Chop roughly and blend to a smooth purée in a blender.
   Use as required.

Handy Tip: If frozen, tomato concasse can last for months.

⸂ **Basic Tomato Sauce** ⸃

Here is the recipe for basic tomato sauce, which can then be enhanced with various ingredients like herbs, vegetables, spices, etc., according to the requirements of various recipes. Can be made in advance and refrigerated for close to two weeks.

Preparation time: 10 minutes. Cooking time: 20 minutes. Makes 1 cup (approx.).

4 large tomatoes
¾ cup finely chopped onions
2 tsp finely chopped garlic
2 tbsp tomato ketchup
1 tbsp cream
1 tsp oregano
1 tbsp olive oil
Salt to taste

1. Blanch the tomatoes in boiling water.
2. Peel, cut into quarters and deseed the tomatoes.
3. Chop them finely and keep the tomato pulp aside.

4. Heat the olive oil in a pan, add the onions and garlic sauté for 3 to 4 minutes.
5. Add the tomatoes, tomato ketchup and salt and sauté for 4 to 5 minutes until the sauce thickens.
6. Add the cream and oregano and mix well.
   Use as required.

Handy Tip: You can make the sauce in advance in large quantities by multiplying the above recipe and refrigerate until required.

ℭ **Tortillas** ℭ

Extremely popular and a part of almost every meal in Mexico, tortillas can be visualised as chapattis made from maize flour.

Preparation time: 15 minutes.   Cooking time: 5 minutes.   Makes 4 tortillas.

½ cup maize flour (*makai ka atta*)
¼ cup plain flour (*maida*)
1 tsp oil
½ tsp salt

Other ingredients
Plain flour for rolling
Oil for cooking

1. Mix the maize flour, plain flour, oil and salt and make soft dough by adding enough warm water.
2. Knead the dough well and keep aside for ½ hour.

3. Knead again and divide the dough into 4 equal portions. Roll out each portion into 125 mm. (5") diameter thin rounds with the help of a little flour.
4. Cook lightly with oil on a *tava* (griddle) and keep aside.
5. Repeat with the remaining 3 portions to make 3 more tortillas.

Healthy Variation:

Healthy Tortillas: Use ½ cup of whole wheat flour instead of maize flour in the above recipe.

◖ **Low Fat Paneer** ◗

Paneer goes low-fat! Try making paneer at home using this recipe and enjoy a low fat version.

Preparation time: 10 minutes.   Cooking time: 10 minutes.
Makes ½ cup (approx.).

2 cups readymade low fat milk (99.9% fat free or doubled tonned)
1 cup whisked low fat curds (*dahi*)

1. Put the milk to boil in a pan. When it starts boiling, add the low fat curds and mix well.
2. Remove from the heat and stir gently until the milk curdles.
3. Strain the curdled milk through a muslin cloth, bring the edges of the cloth together, tie and hang for about ½ hour to allow the whey to drain out.
   Use as required.

Handy Tip: If the milk has not curdled completely in step 2, heat the mixture for a little more time. Whey is very nutritious so try using it innovatively instead of discarding it. It can be used instead of water for kneading dough or can be added to juices and buttermilk.

Mini Series by *Tarla Dalal*

Healthy Breakfast

Healthy Snacks

Healthy
Soups & Salads

Healthy Juices

Fast Foods
Made Healthy

Calcium
Rich Recipes

Iron Rich Recipes

Forever Young Diet

Home Remedies

Low Cholesterol
Recipes